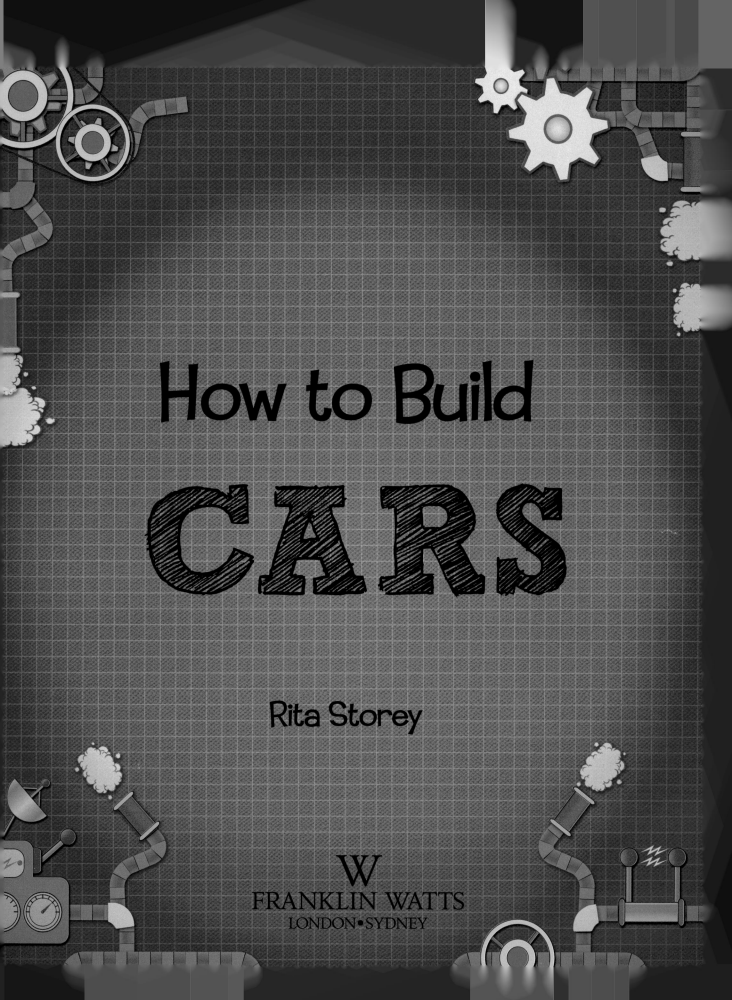

How to Build

CARS

Rita Storey

W
FRANKLIN WATTS
LONDON · SYDNEY

Franklin Watts
First published in Great Britain in 2016 by
The Watts Publishing Group

Credits
Executive editor: Adrian Cole
Packaged by Storeybooks
Design manager: Peter Scoulding
Cover design and illustrations: Cathryn Gilbert

Dewey number 629.2'22
ISBN 978 1 4451 4464 1

Printed in China

Photo credits:
The publishers would like to thank the following for permission to reproduce their
photos: Land Rover MENA; Rob Bulmahn 17; Flock and Siemens 9; Wikimedia
Commons: 4, 5.
Step-by-step photography by Tudor Photography, Banbury.

Every attempt has been made to clear copyright. Should there be any inadvertent
omission please apply to the publisher for rectification.

Franklin Watts
An imprint of
Hachette Children's Group
Part of The Watts Publishing Group
Carmelite House
50 Victoria Embankment
London EC4Y 0DZ

An Hachette UK Company
www.hachette.co.uk

www.franklinwatts.co.uk

CONTENTS

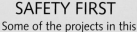

SAFETY FIRST

Some of the projects in this book require scissors, sharp tools or a hot glue gun. When using these things we would recommend that children are supervised by a responsible adult.

About cars

Cars as we know them today were invented in 1885. At first, cars were incredibly expensive as they were handmade. When American car manufacturer, Henry Ford (left), invented the assembly line in 1913, his factory workers were able to produce cars much more quickly - and car prices tumbled. Today, there are over a billion cars on the roads, worldwide.

Car fashions
Over time the shape and colour of cars have changed. These changes reflect the materials and technologies available to produce them, and the fashion of the day.

40s

60s

50s

70s

90s

2000s

80s

Purpose built
Cars are now designed to fit the needs and lifestyles of groups of individuals. Sports utility vehicles (SUVs), sports cars, people carriers, hatchbacks, city cars and supercars are just some of the ranges on offer.

Built for speed

Many cars are built to accelerate quickly and reach speeds much higher than the legal speed limit on the roads. For those who want to drive very fast there are a range of motor sports available. The fastest of these is drag racing with a top speed of 530 kph (330 mph), followed by Formula 1 racing where cars can reach a top speed of almost 370 kph (230 mph).

Built at speed

Not only can modern cars go very fast but they are also built quickly. Using robots for much of the assembly allows manufacturers to assemble a car in approximately 67 seconds.

Cars of the future

Almost all the cars on our roads today run on petrol or diesel. Burning these fuels releases gases, including carbon dioxide, which pollute the atmosphere. Engineers, designers and inventors are searching for ways to design cars that use less fuel or use dual fuel (hybrid cars), electric power, solar power, or some other source of energy.
Self-parking cars are a reality and designers are hard at work on prototypes of self-driving cars. The future of the car looks very exciting.

Before you get started on each of the projects in this book, you'll need to gather together the materials and tools listed in the 'you will need' box. Hopefully you will have most things to hand, but some of the more unusual items can be bought from suppliers listed on page 32.

Balloon car

To make a balloon car you will need:

- corrugated card, 10 cm x 18 cm
- scissors
- ruler
- paint • paintbrush
- 2 x straight plastic drinking straws
- flexible plastic drinking straw
- 4 x plastic bottle tops (the same size)
- offcut of wood
- nail and hammer
- 2 x wooden skewers, trimmed to 14 cm length
- sticky tape
- balloon (blow it up a couple of times to stretch it)

1

Paint the card and leave it to dry.

2

12 CM

Use a ruler and a pair of scissors to cut each straight drinking straw to 12 cm in length.

3

Place a bottle top on the piece of wood. Hold the nail so that the point is exactly in the centre. Tap the nail gently with the hammer to make a hole. Remove the nail. Repeat with the other three bottle tops.

4

5 MM

Push a wooden skewer through the hole in the bottle top so that a 5 mm length pokes through the hole.

5

Thread the wooden skewer through one of the drinking straws.

6

Add a second bottle top, as you did in step 4, to create a car axle. Repeat steps 4–6 using the other skewer, remaining bottle tops and straight drinking straw.

7

3 CM

3 CM

Tape the axles to
the card, 3 cm
from each end.

8

Slide the end of the flexible
drinking straw inside the
balloon, leaving the flexible
end free. Wrap sticky tape
around the straw and the
balloon to join them together.

9

Tape the straw attached to the
balloon onto the body of the
car, with the flexible part of the
straw poking up at one end.

10

Blow through the straw to
inflate the balloon. Pinch
the end of the straw to
stop the air escaping.

11

Place the balloon car
on a smooth surface
and let it go.

Glitch Fix!

Glitch: if the balloon will
not blow up there may be
a gap in the seal between
the balloon and the straw.
Fix: wind more tape
tightly around the join.

Balloon bottle car

This car is quick off the start line.

This balloon bottle car works in exactly the same way as the balloon car on pages 6–7. The car is pushed forward by the air that flows out of the drinking straw as the balloon deflates. As the air rushes out of the balloon, it creates a forward movement called thrust.

To make a balloon bottle car you will need:
- small plastic juice bottle
- scissors (with pointed ends)
- 2 x straight plastic drinking straws
- flexible plastic drinking straw
- 4 x plastic bottle tops
- offcut of wood
- nail and hammer • glue gun
- 2 x wooden skewers, 12 cm long
- balloon (blow it up a couple of times to stretch it)
- sticky tape

1 Ask an adult to use the scissors to make a hole in the side of the plastic bottle, near to the neck.

HOLE

2 Use scissors to trim the straight drinking straws so that they are 10 cm long. Follow steps 3–6 on page 6 to make two pairs of wheels and axles.

⚠️ Ask an adult to supervise when you use the hot glue gun.

3 Hot glue the axles to the body of the bottle, on the opposite side to the hole you made in step 1.

4 Slide the end of the flexible drinking straw into the balloon. Wrap sticky tape around the join.

5 Slide the flexible end of the straw through the hole in the bottle and out of the neck.

Blow through the straw to inflate the balloon. Pinch the end of the straw to prevent air from escaping. Put the balloon bottle car on a smooth surface and let go.

A fair test

Try racing the two types of balloon car (pages 6–9) over a measured distance to see which one goes furthest, fastest and straightest.

To see if you can improve the performance of the winning car, make a second one that is identical except for one change (see right, for suggestions). Race the cars again and record the results.

If the change you made does not improve the performance of the car, or made it worse, change it back and think of another change that might work better. This way you can make your car a race winner.

POWER SOURCE: TRY USING A DIFFERENT SHAPED BALLOON OR A LARGER BALLOON

BODY: TRY USING A LARGER PLASTIC DRINK BOTTLE, A PAPER CUP OR A WAXED JUICE CARTON

WHEELS: TRY USING BIGGER PLASTIC BOTTLE TOPS, OR ATTACHING SANDPAPER STRIPS TO THE WHEELS TO IMPROVE GRIP

AXLES: TRY SPACING THEM FURTHER APART

Is it a car or is it a rocket?

Bloodhound is a supersonic car that will be powered by a jet engine and a rocket. The aim is to break the current world land speed record by reaching speeds in excess of 1,600 kph and, at the same time, inspire a new generation of scientists and engineers.

Find out more about the Bloodhound Project at:

http://www.bloodhoundssc.com/education

Rubber band car

Is this car a wind up?

What makes it move? By winding the chain of rubber bands around the car's axle, you have stored energy in the stretched rubber bands. When you let go of the car, the rubber bands release the energy as they return to their original shape. The energy turns the wheels and the car moves forward.

To make a rubber band car you will need:
- 4 x unwanted CDs
- 4 x plastic bottle tops
- nail and hammer
- offcut of wood
- glue gun
- rubber washing-up glove
- scissors
- 2 x wooden dowels, 5 mm x 18 cm
- cardboard tube from inside a kitchen roll, painted red and left to dry
- 6 x rubber bands • sticky tape

⚠️ Ask an adult to supervise when you use the hot glue gun.

1 Use the nail and hammer to make a hole in each bottle top (see step 3 on page 6) for the dowels to fit through. Use the glue gun to stick a bottle top to the centre of each CD to make four wheels.

2 Cut four 1-cm wide pieces from the sleeve of the washing-up glove. Stretch one of the pieces of rubber glove around the edge of each CD wheel. This will help them to grip the floor as they turn.

3 Carefully use the nail to make two holes opposite each other, 4 cm from each end of the cardboard tube that forms the body of the car. Push the dowels through the holes. The dowels need to be able to turn freely in the holes.

4 Push the free ends of the dowels through the centre of each CD wheel. Glue them in place with the glue gun.

5

Place two rubber bands on top of each other so that they overlap as shown. Lift the section of the rubber band that is underneath (A), over the other rubber band and tuck it under the opposite side (B).

Pull the loop tight. Repeat to join the rest of the rubber bands to make a chain.

6

Loop one end of the rubber band chain over one of the dowel axles inside the car. Feed the rest of the chain through the loop and pull it tight.

7

Pass the end of the rubber band chain through the car tube and out the opposite end.

8

Use a piece of sticky tape to fix the other end of the rubber band chain to the second dowel axle. Turn the axle to wind up the chain of rubber bands until they are taut.

9

Place the rubber band car on a flat surface and let it go.

Battery fan car

Switch on the fan to see this car whizz along the ground!

What makes it move? The fan is powered by two small batteries. When the fan is switched on, the blades spin, drawing in air and then pushing it out again and away from the back of the car, which pushes the car forwards.

To make a battery fan car you will need:

- cardboard crisp tube, including its plastic lid
- piece of wrapping paper the same length as the tube, and long enough to wrap around it with a 1-cm overlap
- scissors with pointed ends
- glue gun
- 4 x large plastic lids (all the same size)
- nail and hammer
- offcut of wood
- 2 x straight plastic drinking straws
- 2 x wooden skewers
- a small battery-operated fan

1

Wrap the wrapping paper around the cardboard tube and glue it in place where it overlaps.

2

Use the nail and hammer to create a hole in the centre of each plastic lid (see step 3 on page 6) to make four wheels.

3

3 CM   1 CM   3 CM

Ask an adult to use the point of the scissors to make a hole, 3 cm from each end of the tube. Make another pair of holes on the opposite side of the tube.
Push a drinking straw through each pair of holes. Cut them to length, so that 1 cm of drinking straw sticks out on either side of the crisp tube. They need to fit the holes tightly. If yours are loose, use the glue gun to fix them in place.

4

5 MM

Push the wooden skewers through the straws. Trim the ends with scissors so that 5 mm of each skewer sticks out of each end of the straws.

12

5

Ask an adult to supervise when you use the hot glue gun.

6

Push the wheels onto the ends of the wooden skewers. Use the glue gun to put a blob of glue on the end of each skewer. (The skewers need to move freely inside the drinking straws.)

Remove the lid from the end of the car. Use the glue gun to stick the battery fan to the outside of the lid so that the blades overhang.

7

Fix the lid back onto the end of the car so that the blades of the fan are at the top.

8

Place your battery fan car on a smooth surface and switch it on. Away it goes!

DIRECTION THE AIR TRAVELS

DIRECTION THE CAR TRAVELS

Propeller car

A small electric motor powers this speedy propeller car.

How does the propeller move the car? The plastic propeller is connected to a small electric motor, powered by a battery. The motor drives the propeller, which spins round and round, grabbing air and throwing it out backwards, creating a thrust force that moves the car forwards.

To make this propeller car you will need:

- medium-sized cylindrical plastic drink bottle with its lid
- ruler and felt-tip pen • scissors
- 1.5–3 v small electric motor (available from electronics suppliers – see page 32)
- battery connector
- 4 x drink bottle tops (must be identical)
- nail and hammer
- offcut of wood
- glue gun • 2 x straight plastic drinking straws
- 2 x wooden skewers
- medium-sized cuboid-shaped plastic drink bottle
- battery holder and 2 x AA batteries

1

Use the ruler to measure 6 cm from the top of the cylindrical bottle. Make a mark on the bottle. Cut across the top of the bottle.

2

Take care as the plastic edge is sharp. Use scissors to make cuts 15 mm apart, cutting from the outer edge towards the bottle's neck.

3

Push the top of the bottle against a hard surface, so that the pieces fan out and bend back.

4

Twist each of the cut pieces to the right, as shown, to create a propeller shape.

5

TERMINALS

SPINDLE

Connect the ends of the wires on the battery connector to the two terminals on the electric motor.

6

Take the bottle top that fits the bottle you used to make the propeller and use a nail and a hammer (see step 3 on page 6) to make a hole in it. Push the spindle through the hole.

7

⚠️

Ask an adult to supervise when you use the hot glue gun.

Use a blob of hot glue to secure the spindle to the inside of the bottle top. Leave to dry.

8

Screw the propeller you made in steps 1–4 into the bottle top with the motor on it.

9

Follow steps 3–6 on page 6 to make wheels and axles for the car, using four bottle tops, two drinking straws and two wooden skewers.

10

Glue the axles onto one side of the cuboid drink bottle to create a car body with wheels.

11 Position the motor-powered propeller so that it juts out over the back of the car body and can spin freely. If it touches the ground, see Glitch Fix box, below. Use the glue gun to stick it in place. Leave it to dry.

12 Glue the battery pack to the top of the car body. Connect the battery terminal to the connector.

Glitch Fix!
Glitch: the propeller touches the ground.
Fix: glue a bottle top to the top of the bottle. Glue the motor onto the bottle top to raise it up.

Glitch Fix!
Glitch: the car goes backwards.
Fix: swap the connectors on the motor over to the opposite side, or twist the propeller blades a quarter turn in the opposite direction.

13 Place your car on a smooth surface and watch it race away.

Car design - basics

Large teams of designers work together to produce a new car.
Each team will focus on one element of the design.

Body Car designers think very carefully about the shape of a new car – its body. They want the car to move through the air as smoothly as possible, so they pay great attention to aerodynamics. Aerodynamics is the study of the way air moves around objects. Smooth, flat, low-to-the-ground cars move through the air much more easily than boxy, tall cars, and use less fuel as a result.

Engine The fuel that will drive the car is an important factor in designing a new car. Almost all cars today have an internal combustion engine. The engine works by burning a mixture of fuel (petrol or diesel) and air inside a cylinder containing a piston (a metal rod). This creates an explosion that moves the piston down, which turns a crankshaft linked to the wheels.

To watch a video showing how a car engine works, go to:
http://www.sciencekids.co.nz/videos/engineering/carengine.html

Gears Gears allow the wheels to move at variable speeds. A low gear allows the wheels to turn slowly but with a strong force. So a low gear is good for climbing hills or getting the car moving from a standstill. If the car is moving on a flat surface and does not need so much power, then a higher gear allows the engine to put more of its power into making speed.

WHEN THESE GEARS TURN, THE SMALLER ONE WILL GO FASTER AND TURN MORE TIMES THAN THE LARGER ONE.

To watch a video showing how gears work,

Car design - safety and comfort

As well as designing cars that look great and drive well, car designers and engineers build in some or all of the features below. These will ensure that their cars are safe and comfortable to drive.

CRUMPLE ZONES
Areas at the front, back and sides of a car are designed to crumple to absorb the impact in a collision and offer protection to the occupants.

AIRBAGS
Up to four airbags at the front and sides inflate to help reduce the impact on occupants during a collision.

SIDE IMPACT BARS
Strengthened bars along the side of the car help reduce the effects of a side impact on occupants involved in a collision.

AIR CONDITIONING
Clean air of the correct temperature is important to keep the occupants comfortable and the driver alert.

ABS BRAKES
An anti-lock braking system (ABS) prevents skidding and allows the driver to retain control in the event of a skid.

SEAT BELTS
In many countries, wearing a seat belt in a car is required by law. They keep the wearer in their seat and stop them from hitting the windscreen or the seat in front. Wearing a seatbelt can reduce your chance of dying in the event of a car crash by 50 per cent.

COLLAPSIBLE STEERING COLUMN
The column that the steering wheel is attached to is designed to collapse if there is an accident. This is to stop it hurting the driver if they are thrown forward.

Car interior People may spend many hours in their car so it is vital that they are comfortable. Car seats are designed to give support and comfort to the occupants and dashboard controls are placed within reach of the driver, in order to prevent accidents. The science behind these decisions is called ergonomics. Car seats, steering wheels and headrests are all adjustable to suit people of all heights and sizes.

Bottle racer

Use light materials to make this speedy model racing car.

How does it move? The bottle racer's small electric motor drives a spindle – which is connected to one of the bottle racer's wheel axles. As the spindle spins, it drives the wheels round and moves the car forward.

To make a bottle racer you will need:
- plastic drink bottle (with a pull-up cap that allows the liquid out)
- craft knife
- 4 x pull-up caps from plastic drink bottles, one with the lid
- 2 x wooden skewers, 10 cm long
- 2 x straight plastic drinking straws, 8 cm long
- glue gun
- scissors
- empty, or partly empty, ballpoint pen refill
- 1.5–3 v small electric motor (available from electronics suppliers – see page 32)
- battery connector
- battery pack
- scraps of foam board
- sticky tape
- small rubber band

1 Ask an adult to use the craft knife to cut the central section out of the bottle.

2 ⚠️ Ask an adult to supervise when you use the hot glue gun.

Put a blob of hot glue inside one of the plastic bottle caps. Push the end of a wooden skewer into the glue. Hold it upright until the glue begins to set and leave it to set hard. Repeat with a second bottle top and skewer.

3 Fill these bottle tops with more glue from the glue gun. Leave to harden.

4 Slide the skewers with the bottle caps attached inside the drinking straws to make axles for your car.

5 Ask an adult to use the point of the scissors to make a hole on each side of the bottle, near the bottle's neck. The holes should be the same height from the worktop and slightly larger than the diameter of the straws.

6 Repeat step 5, but this time make the holes at the other end of the bottle but level with those at the front.

OUTER CAP

7 Push the drinking straw axles through the holes in the bottle. Put the outer cap back on the wheel on the left, nearest to the neck of the bottle.

8 Add a wheel to the other side of each axle by putting a blob of hot glue inside each of the remaining bottle caps and hold it in place on the end of the wooden skewers. Take care not to glue the bottle cap to the drinking straws. Leave to dry and harden.

9 Cut the pen end off the refill. Put a blob of glue onto the spindle of the electric motor. Push the plastic refill tube onto the spindle. Leave to dry.

CUT

SPINDLE

10

CONNECTOR

TERMINALS

Connect the ends of the wires on the battery connector to the two terminals on the electric motor.

11

HOLE

Make a hole in the side of the bottle. It should be level with the top of the front left wheel.

12

Turn the car round. Working from inside the body of the bottle racer, slide the motor's spindle tube through the hole you created in step 11. Cut some small pieces of foam board and place them under the motor until the spindle is level. Use the hot glue gun to fix the foam board in place and glue the motor on top.

FOAM BOARD

13

Glue the bottom of the battery pack alongside the motor. Make sure that it does not touch the wheel axle. Leave enough space to connect the battery to the motor using the connector.

SPACE

BATTERY PACK

14

Turn the car around. Wrap sticky tape tightly around the spindle tube.

15

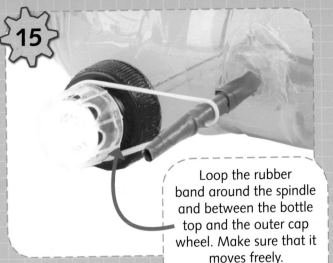

Loop the rubber band around the spindle and between the bottle top and the outer cap wheel. Make sure that it moves freely.

16

Connect the battery terminals. As you do so the wheels will begin to spin.

17

Place your car on a smooth surface and watch it go. Disconnect the battery to turn off the motor.

Glitch Fix!

Glitch: the rubber band falls off.

Fix: wrap more tape around the end of the spindle.

Design and test

The battery and motor that provide the power for this car can be used to propel a variety of different car designs.

Using different materials, design, make and test another car powered by the battery and motor.

Car with gears

See how gear wheels transfer energy in this model car.

What's going on here? The gear box kit includes an electric motor powered by batteries. The spindle on the motor is attached to a gear wheel attached to a metal axle, which becomes the back axle of this car. When you turn the motor on, it turns the back axle of the car, making it move forwards.

To make this car with gears you will need:
- pencil and thin white paper (for tracing the template)
- scissors • A3 sheet of foam board
- black acrylic paint
- orange acrylic paint
- paintbrush • silver duct tape
- ruler • glue gun
- straight plastic drinking straw
- 4 x plastic lids from crisp cans or coffee tins
- wooden skewer, trimmed to13-cm length
- nail and hammer • offcut of wood
- 3 v worm drive gear box kit, including battery holder (available from electronics suppliers – see page 32) • 2 x AA batteries
- 2 x thin pieces of card, 1 cm x 7 cm

1 Trace and cut out the template on page 29 and use it to cut two car shapes from the foam board. Paint the foam car shapes. The design needs to be on the side that will face out. Paint the other side black. Leave to dry.

2 Use the paper template again to cut two window shapes out of silver duct tape. Stick them to the foam board car shapes.

3 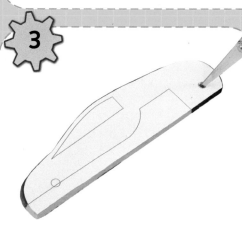 Use the paper template to make two marks on each of the foam board cars. Use the point of the scissors to make a small hole at each mark.

⚠️ Ask an adult to supervise when you use the hot glue gun.

4 4 CM

1.5 CM

Cut a rectangle of foam board, 6.5 cm x 17 cm. Glue along one long edge and fix it to the black side of one of the foam board cars, 1.5 cm from the bottom edge and 4 cm from the back edge.

5

Paint the rims of the plastic lids black and the centres orange. Make a hole in the centre of each lid using the nail and hammer (see step 3 on page 6).

6

Push the wooden skewer through a hole in one of the plastic lids so that 2 mm of the end pokes through. Glue in place.

7

Using the photo as reference, take the worm drive gear box with the metal axle attached to it and push the axle through the hole in the foam board car. Slide on one of the lid wheels. Glue the bottom of the gear box casing to the rectangular foam board, positioning it at the back of the car. Glue the bottom of the battery holder to the central section of the foam board.

8

Spread glue on the free edge of the rectangular foam board. Guide the other end of the metal axle through the small hole in the second foam board car and hold the foam board pieces together until they set. Leave to dry.

9

Push the drinking straw through the remaining holes at the front of the foam board car shapes. Slide the wooden skewer with a wheel attached into the straw. Add another wheel to the free end of the skewer. Glue in place.

Slide the remaining wheel onto the metal back axle. Put a blob of hot glue in the centre of each wheel to fix them all in place.

10

Cut a rectangle of foam board 8 cm x 2.5 cm.
Paint it and leave it to dry.

Cover the two pieces of thin
card with silver duct tape.

Glue the pieces of silver
card on either side of the
foam board, to create
a spoiler.

Glue the spoiler onto the outside
of the back of the car at a
45 degree angle.

11

Connect the metal ends of the red
and black wires to the two battery
terminals. Bend the metal wires back
to keep them in place.

12

Place the car on a smooth surface.
Switch it on and watch the gear
wheel turn the back axle.

Solar car

How does it work? The solar panel on the top of the car is coated in a special material that absorbs sunlight and converts it into electrical energy. This energy travels down the wires to drive the motor, which is attached to a propeller. The propeller whizzes round, sucking in air and pushing it out backwards, which moves the car forwards.

To make this solar car you will need:
- pencil and thin white paper (for tracing the template)
- scissors • ruler
- 2 x pieces of foam board, 8 cm x 21 cm • glue gun • paint and paintbrush • metal skewer
- 2 x straight plastic drinking straws
- 2 x wooden skewers
- micro motor (4 v solar micro motor 47,000 rpm), propeller and solar panel kit (available from electronics suppliers – see page 32)
- small screwdriver
- 2 x polystyrene balls, 4 cm in diameter
- 2 x polystyrene balls, 1.5 cm in diameter

⚠ Ask an adult to supervise when you use the hot glue gun.

1

Use the paper and pencil to trace the template on page 29. Cut it out and use it to cut out two triangular shapes from each piece of foam board.

2

Glue the four foam triangles together, matching up the edges. Paint. Leave to dry.

3

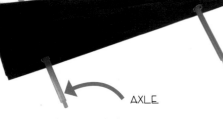

AXLE

Use the metal skewer to make two holes through the foam board triangles. Use the paper template from step 1 to help you choose the right place. Push the drinking straws through the holes and slide the wooden skewers through the straws to create two axles.

4

Place the foam car body on the work surface. Push a 4-cm-diameter polystyrene ball onto each end of the back axle. Make sure that the foam ball does not touch the drinking straw.

Push a 1.5-cm-diameter polystyrene ball onto each end of the front axle. Make sure that all the wheels turn freely on the axles.

5 Use the screwdriver to undo the screws in the plastic connection box a little, leaving a small space under the tip of each screw.

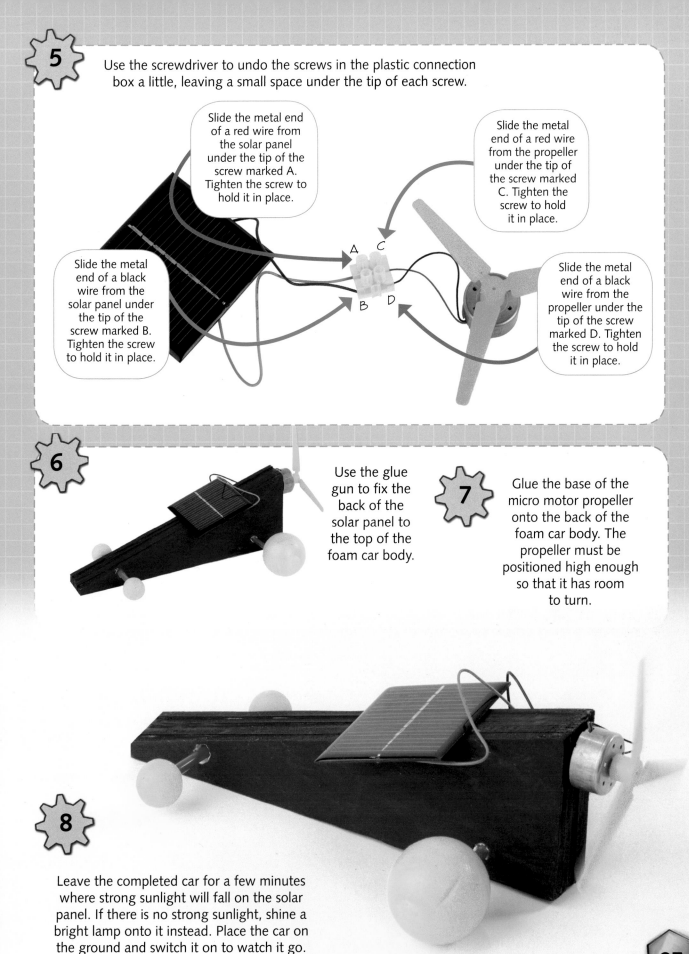

Slide the metal end of a red wire from the solar panel under the tip of the screw marked A. Tighten the screw to hold it in place.

Slide the metal end of a red wire from the propeller under the tip of the screw marked C. Tighten the screw to hold it in place.

Slide the metal end of a black wire from the solar panel under the tip of the screw marked B. Tighten the screw to hold it in place.

Slide the metal end of a black wire from the propeller under the tip of the screw marked D. Tighten the screw to hold it in place.

6 Use the glue gun to fix the back of the solar panel to the top of the foam car body.

7 Glue the base of the micro motor propeller onto the back of the foam car body. The propeller must be positioned high enough so that it has room to turn.

8 Leave the completed car for a few minutes where strong sunlight will fall on the solar panel. If there is no strong sunlight, shine a bright lamp onto it instead. Place the car on the ground and switch it on to watch it go.

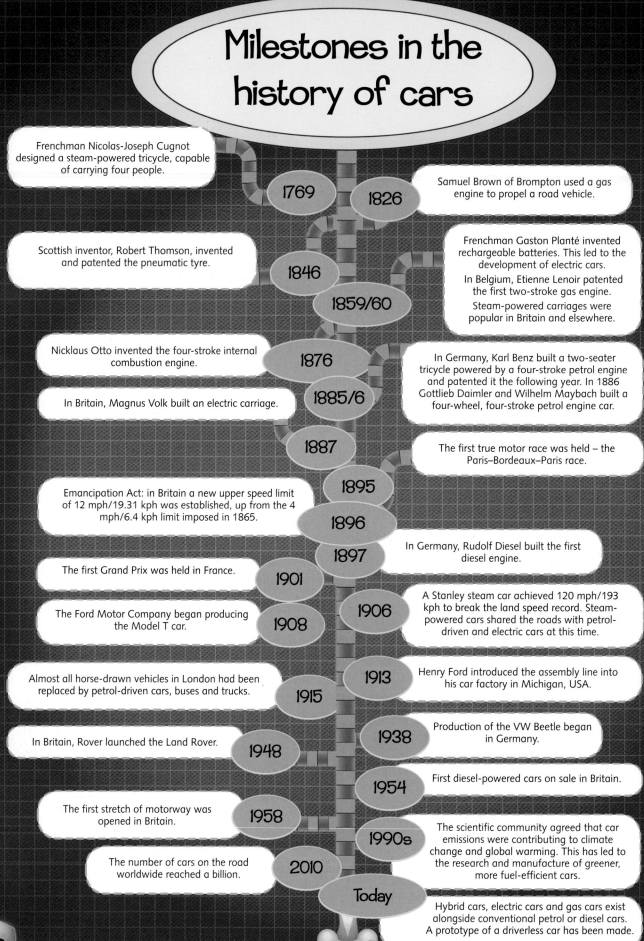

Milestones in the history of cars

Frenchman Nicolas-Joseph Cugnot designed a steam-powered tricycle, capable of carrying four people.

1769

1826

Samuel Brown of Brompton used a gas engine to propel a road vehicle.

Scottish inventor, Robert Thomson, invented and patented the pneumatic tyre.

1846

1859/60

Frenchman Gaston Planté invented rechargeable batteries. This led to the development of electric cars.
In Belgium, Etienne Lenoir patented the first two-stroke gas engine.
Steam-powered carriages were popular in Britain and elsewhere.

Nicklaus Otto invented the four-stroke internal combustion engine.

1876

1885/6

In Germany, Karl Benz built a two-seater tricycle powered by a four-stroke petrol engine and patented it the following year. In 1886 Gottlieb Daimler and Wilhelm Maybach built a four-wheel, four-stroke petrol engine car.

In Britain, Magnus Volk built an electric carriage.

1887

The first true motor race was held – the Paris–Bordeaux–Paris race.

1895

Emancipation Act: in Britain a new upper speed limit of 12 mph/19.31 kph was established, up from the 4 mph/6.4 kph limit imposed in 1865.

1896

1897

In Germany, Rudolf Diesel built the first diesel engine.

The first Grand Prix was held in France.

1901

1906

A Stanley steam car achieved 120 mph/193 kph to break the land speed record. Steam-powered cars shared the roads with petrol-driven and electric cars at this time.

The Ford Motor Company began producing the Model T car.

1908

1913

Henry Ford introduced the assembly line into his car factory in Michigan, USA.

Almost all horse-drawn vehicles in London had been replaced by petrol-driven cars, buses and trucks.

1915

1938

Production of the VW Beetle began in Germany.

In Britain, Rover launched the Land Rover.

1948

1954

First diesel-powered cars on sale in Britain.

The first stretch of motorway was opened in Britain.

1958

1990s

The scientific community agreed that car emissions were contributing to climate change and global warming. This has led to the research and manufacture of greener, more fuel-efficient cars.

The number of cars on the road worldwide reached a billion.

2010

Today

Hybrid cars, electric cars and gas cars exist alongside conventional petrol or diesel cars. A prototype of a driverless car has been made.

Templates

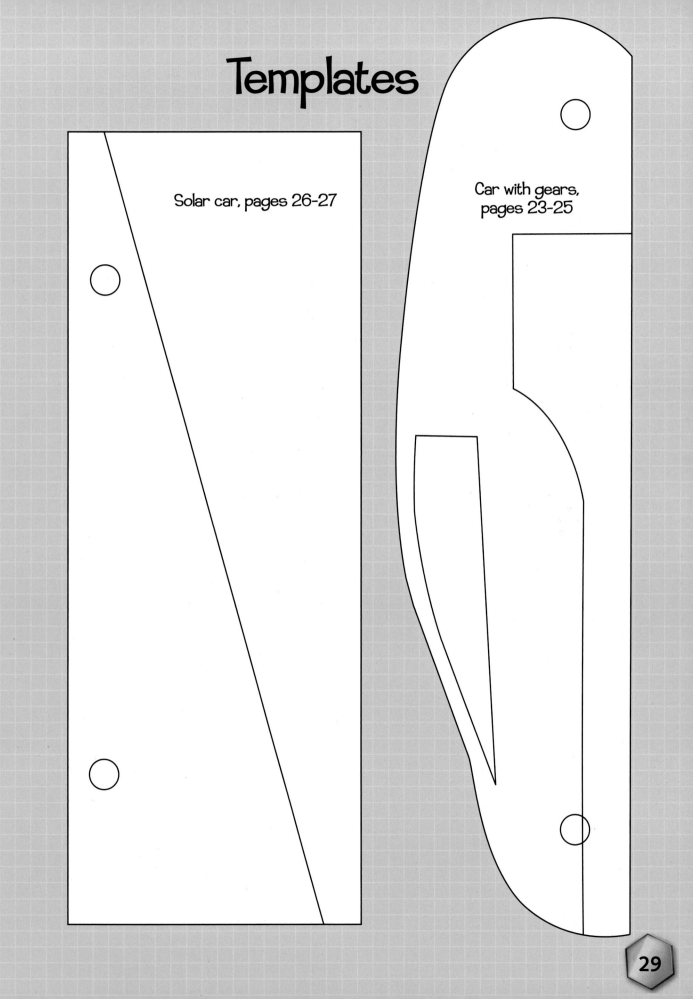

Solar car, pages 26-27

Car with gears, pages 23-25

Glossary

Aerodynamics The study of how objects move through air.

Assembly line A line of workers and machines performing a particular task as they assemble a product, which is moving in front of them inside a factory.

Atmosphere The layer of protective gases that surrounds planet Earth.

Climate change Changes in the world's weather that most people believe are a result of human activity on Earth.

Crankshaft A long metal rod that helps the engine turn the wheels.

Diesel A liquid fuel derived from oil.

Drag racing A type of motor sport in which two vehicles compete side-by-side to be the fastest to cover a short distance from a standing start.

Dual-fuel car A car with an engine capable of running on two fuels. One fuel is usually petrol or diesel and the other is a less polluting fuel, such as natural gas or hydrogen.

Eco Not harming the environment.

Electric car A car powered by rechargeable batteries.

Energy The ability to do work. It comes in several forms, including heat, light, chemical energy and electricity.

Force A push or a pull.

Formula 1 The most popular form of world motor racing.

Fuel efficiency The way an engine works, to waste as little fuel as possible.

Gear One of a set of toothed wheels that work together to alter the relationship between the (car) engine and the speed of the driven parts (the wheels).

Hatchback A car with a door at the back that opens upwards, giving full access to the boot for loading.

Internal combustion engine An engine that generates moving power by mixing fuel and air inside the engine to create an explosion that moves a piston or pistons, joined to other moving parts.

Newton, Sir Isaac (1642-1727) British scientist and mathematician, best known for his discoveries relating to gravity, the laws of motion and the science of light.

People carrier A car with three rows of seats, allowing the vehicle to carry more passengers than a normal car.

Petrol A liquid fuel derived from oil.

Propeller A revolving shaft with two or more angled blades attached to it, used for propelling a boat or aircraft.

Prototype A first or early version of a design or vehicle, from which others will be developed.

Solar Relating to the Sun. Solar power is the conversion of sunlight into electrical energy.

Sports utility vehicle (SUV) A four-wheel-drive car capable of driving in on-road and off-road driving conditions.

Steam car A car driven by steam power, generated in a boiler.

Supercar A high-performance sports car.

Thrust A pushing force that moves something forward.

Further information

For information about brakes, lights, fuel, horn, tyres and
windscreen wipers:
http://www.funkidslive.com/features/fun-kids-guide-to-cars/

All about the Bloodhound model rocket car challenge:

http://www.bloodhoundssc.com/news/bloodhound-model-rocket
-car-challenge

Use this link to find out how your school can take part in a world
record attempt for the fastest rocket-powered model car:

http://www.guinnessworldrecords.com/news/2015/8/video-
bloodhound-project-how-you-can-take-part-in-a-world-record-
attempt-for-391281

Construct a car at:

http://www.mylearning.org/intermediate-interactive.
asp?type=4&journeyid=337

What do you think the car of the future should look like?:

http://www.fastcoexist.com/3033618/what-kids-think-the-car-of-the-
future-should-look-like-is-awesome

Animations and information about how a car is made:
https://www.toyota.co.jp/en/kids/car/test.html

Index

Crafts and parts suppliers

Craft shops, art shops, office suppliers and stationery shops will sell most of the materials you will need to build the models in this book – and you will be able to use materials you have at home or at school.

A good online craft store is: www.bakerross.co.uk

This electronics supplier sells electric motors and other related components:
www.maplin.co.uk

Note to parents and teachers: every effort has been made
by the Publishers to ensure that these websites are suitable for children,
that they are of the highest educational value, and that
they contain no inappropriate or offensive material.
However, because of the nature of the Internet, it is
impossible to guarantee that the contents of these
sites will not be altered.
We strongly advise that Internet access is
supervised by a responsible adult.